True North

Navigating Our Way in This Digital Age

Bill McEwen

2014

Introduction

He had just turned fifty one when he died suddenly and very unexpectedly just as he was beginning his fall harvest. He owned the land adjacent to mine, was my closest neighbor, and our respective families have had deep roots in this soil for generations. We buried him there on his farm on a beautiful knoll overlooking the Duck River. It was to be a full moon night on the 30th of September 2012.

All of us have had "wake up" calls in our life and if we're paying attention, these experiences can add much value to our journey. In addition to my neighbor's sudden death, my Vietnam experience served as one of those calls and has influenced my life. That experience also sharpened my vision as to what is really important. As a young Marine officer, I had much to learn, and the war would prove to be a good teacher if I would only pay attention. I can vividly remember when the lessons began. It was January 21st 1968 at 5:30 am when the first rocket slammed into our perimeter not far from my location. That round marked the beginning of the siege at Khe Sanh which in retrospect turned out to be a very historic event and one of the turning points of the Vietnam War. While there during the siege, surrounded by North Vietnamese troops, and under constant attack, the lessons began to unfold: I learned that the difference between life and death is seconds and millimeters...the sacred geometry of chance and luck; that the only thing really within my control was my mind and how I chose to respond to my circumstances (and sometime that was questionable!); that the span of my life was simply the time between inhaling and exhaling. What revelations!

Introduction

When I had my first operation and was diagnosed with pseudomyxoma peritonei a very rare form of cancer in January 2012, my focus was transformed into a laser and taken to a whole new level. I was once again reminded of my Vietnam epiphany. A year later in January 2013 after another major surgery, the lessons became very clear and I really understood. When the universe is moving us toward a new consciousness, we need to recognize the winds of change and move with them instead of clinging to what is already past. I learned that what is required of me now is that I be fully present to each moment, to each new experience as it comes, and that I engage with it as completely as I can. And this can only happen one breath at a time. I didn't really say this to myself; it was nothing as conscious as that. It was if my whole being turned, and looked, and moved toward the experience.

If one is to live an effective life and maximize their human potential, there are certain natural laws or principles which are paramount. The following are a few examples: all forms of life are connected, and we are all part of an interdependent web of life; everything changes, and trying to hang on to changing phenomena makes us anxious, uneasy, unhappy, and causes much needless stress; our thoughts and perceptions determine OUR reality, but they are not necessarily THE reality; everyone has the power to choose their response to any given circumstance; the present moment is all we have. The many principles dispersed throughout this book are my attempt to share only some of those laws which I have found to be of great significance. I have studied and attempted to internalize each of the quotations on the following pages; they

Introduction

represent the best that I have to offer at this particular juncture of my life. When one crosses the threshold from mere "believing" to actually "knowing", then things become real. My life has taught me that all of these concepts are self evident, self validating, timeless, and universal. Great truths have always been available if only we would take the opportunity to rediscover them. This book will only serve as a gentle reminder for many of the things which you already know but which have perhaps been pushed aside by your lifestyle. I cannot tell you anything that deep within that you don't already know. When you have reached a certain stage of inner connectedness and awareness, you will recognize the truth when you hear it.

Why the title "True North" for this book? A brief explanation might be helpful. One definition of a compass is "an instrument for showing direction especially one with a magnetic needle always pointing north. Perhaps as you read this book, you will come to understand to an even greater degree that certain principles or natural laws are like a compass: they are always pointing the way. And if we know how to read, internalize, and apply them, we won't get lost, confused, or fooled by all the conflicting voices in our world. Because the compass represents the many directions which our life can take and as the digital age continues to accelerate, it is imperative that we all work to develop and align our lives with deep respect for "True North" principles. The "N" engraved in the rock along with an aligned compass pointing "North" was chosen for this book's front cover because of its profound symbolism, In addition, that rock, compass, and the surrounding prayer

Introduction

circle are located on a very special and "sacred hill" here on my farm. No matter what happens in a world of uncertainty, these principles which have stood the test of time will always point us in the right direction.

Before we get too far, you need to understand what I mean when I discuss natural laws. To me a natural law looks like the following: "a fundamental pattern of nature and life that human experience and life have shown to be valid. They describe things as they really are as opposed to how we think they are or wish they were." Whether we agree with them or not, these laws ultimately govern our lives and operate independent of our wishes. By becoming aware of them and aligning our lives with them, we can begin to maximize our potential and raise our levels of consciousness. If we ignore them or fight them, we will only fail and make ourselves and others miserable.

I encourage you to look at this book as only a signpost which might lead you to your own deeper reality. Just as it has been for me, it will only be through your own courage and willingness to explore both your inner and outer landscape that you will begin to find some answers and creative solutions to the issues in your life. My suggestion for getting the most from this book would be to spend a day or more with each quotation. I suggest living with it, thinking deeply about it, and reflecting on the content. Allow the book to do its work, to challenge you, and perhaps to awaken you from some of your old ways of repetitive and conditioned thinking. Mere words can never explain reality. Only your direct experience enables you to discover the truth for yourself. This book is merely a

Introduction

vehicle which describes some fundamental truths. It's like a raft that carries you to the other shore. The raft is needed but it's not the other shore. The finger is needed to know where to look for the moon, but if you mistake the finger for the moon, you will never know the real moon.

As I mentioned in my first book, "Reflections", timing plays a big role in all our lives, and writing this book has been no exception. It represents my own discoveries and the essence of my thinking at this particular juncture of my life. My purpose in sharing these thoughts is to encourage others so that they may also have a direct experience of reality. In doing so, they will raise their level of consciousness and continue to maximize their potential. However, there's much that can never be conveyed in written words, and the following pages only represent a small portion of my discovered truths. This book waited patiently for the right time…and there is no time except "THE PRESENT!"

As I said in my earlier book, I do not remember or at the time simply failed to note the source for some of this material, and I accept full responsibility for that. If there happens to be some repetition or overlap from my first book, so be it. It simply means that a particular theme, passage, or quotation contains much energy and resonates strongly with me. This book is not intended for publication. I simply want to share it as a gift to friends and to those whose paths I may cross. And if by chance individuals find some meaning and value on these pages, I encourage them to "pass it forward" and share with their family and friends.

Introduction

Finally, I trust that this book will find its way to those who are ready to accept its message. For others it may only represent a seed planted which in time will merge with that seed of enlightment which we all carry within. My deepest gratitude goes to friends, teachers, masters, students, authors, and poets whose wisdom has graced my path. And if, by chance, that I'm able to see a bit further down the road, it's simply because I've stood on their shoulders. My special thanks and gratitude go to all of you who have encouraged me to write.

True North

When it's over, I want to say: all my life I was a bridesmaid married to amazement. I was the bride's groom, taking the world into my arms. I don't want to wonder if I have made of my life something particular and real. I don't want to find myself sighing and frightened or full of argument. I don't want to end up simply having visited this world.

Mary Oliver

Today was another special day: bluebirds were nesting in my boxes, and I planted five oak trees. Perhaps and in addition, I provided a kindness for some future generation and for some faces which I will never see.

Bill McEwen April 14, 2014

Time is different for a tree than for a man. Sun and soil and water, these are the things that an oak and wierwood understands, not days and years and centuries. For men time is a river. We are trapped in its flow, hurtling from past to present, always in the same direction. The lives of trees are different. They root and grow and die in one place, and the river does not move them. The oak is the acorn and the acorn is the oak.

George R.R. Martin

True North

Do you know that when you look at a tree and say: that is an oak tree or a banyan tree, the naming of the tree which is botanical knowledge, has so conditioned your mind that the word comes between you and actually seeing the tree? To come in contact with the tree, you have to put your hand on it, and the word will not help you touch it.

Jiddu Krishnamurti

We abuse land because we view it as a commodity belonging to us. When we see land as a community to which we belong, we may begin to use it with love and respect.

Aldo Leopold

One of the questions which I've often asked myself: how can I live my life where my conscious is consistent with my actions?

Bill McEwen

There are two kinds of suffering: physical pain and mental suffering.

Mirka Knaster

True North

If you want to look and feel old, hate someone; if you want to look young and feel young, have forgiveness in your heart.

Louis Zamperini

In the end it's up to the man what he becomes, and none of those other things matter. In horses, dogs, and men it's character that counts.

Louis L'Lamour

Your habits are what you choose them to be. To modify a habit you must consciously choose to change it and to accept the hard work necessary to do so.

Charles Duhigg

Remembering that I'll be dead soon is probably the most important tool that I've ever encountered to help me make the big choices in life.

Bill McEwen

The older I get the more I see how much motivation matters.

Bill McEwen

True North

Twenty year old lovemaking and seventy year old lovemaking are completely different. Twenty year old turkey hunting and seventy year old turkey hunting are the same.

Tom Kelly

I do not think that either morality or wellness can be legislated or can arise from anything external. Both are internal and arise from conscious choices.

Bill McEwen

The human body is surrounded by something that I call a life field. I suspect that this universal life force may well be another name for God or the Universal Creator.

Robert Fulford

A woman who has trapped her game has a different way about her than one who is still on the stalk.

Louis L' Lamour

Nature is the teacher of all teachers.

Will McEwen

True North

I am no longer a captive or a slave to my thoughts or my thinking. I can consciously choose to move beyond and be a "witnessing presence."

Bill McEwen

The longer I live, the more I realize that simplicity is the ultimate sophistication. Simplicity comes from conquering complexities, not ignoring them.

Bill McEwen

I've noticed that when people come here to stay at "the cabin" it usually takes 2-3 days for them to dispel the clutter from their minds and to settle the scattered energy from their bodies. The compulsive demands of the clock and our digital age do not release their grip easily on the mind and body.

Bill McEwen

If you understand, things are just as they are; if you don't understand, things are just as they are.

Zen Quote

True North

The great way is not difficult if we don't pick and choose.

John Tarrant

The perfection of life with a gun dog, like the perfection of an autumn, is disturbing because you know even as it begins it must end. Time bestows the gift and steals it in the process.

George Bird Evans

Salvation is now. We have a tendency to point ourselves backward or forward in time, but the Gospels say we are either letting Jesus save us now or we are not letting him save us at all. It's called the always available grace of the present moment. It's the first word Jesus preaches: "The time is now! The kingdom is present and here. Turn around. Believe the Good News." In these four phrases we have the summation of all of Jesus' teaching. It's nothing esoteric or pseudo-mystical, just the infinite nature of now.

Richard Rohr

The path around our home is also the ground of awakening.

Thich Nhat Hanh

True North

When your mind begins to slow down, that's when the power of intuition and experiential wisdom begins to kick in and replace all the "monkey chatter."

Bill McEwen

You are the sky. The clouds are what happens, what comes and goes.

Eckhart Tolle

The awareness of bodily sensations is critical in changing functional and emotional states.

Stephen Levine

If every eight year old child were taught meditation, we would eliminate violence in the world in one generation.

The Dali Lama

Beyond right thinking and wrong thinking, there is a field. I will meet you there.

Rumi

True North

I practice meditation to notice the first redbud blooms or the small purple flowers growing by the side of the creek which I otherwise might miss.

Bill McEwen

Well being depends on the maintenance and relationship between the various bodily systems.

Robert Fulford

If you bring forth what is within you, it will save you; if you do not bring forth what is within you, it will destroy you.

Gnostic Gospel of Thomas

The intuitive mind is a sacred gift, and the rational mind is a faithful servant. We have created a society that honors the servant and has forgotten the gift.

Albert Einstein

What is to give light must endure burning.

Viktor Frankl

True North

Behind the restless movement of the mind is the stillness of being, the stillness that has no name, no reputation, nothing to protect. It is the natural mind.

Stephen Levine

We do not find the meaning of life by ourselves alone. We find it with another.

Thomas Merton

We say that the hour of death cannot be forecast, but when we say this we imagine that hour as placed in an obscure future. It never occurs to us that it has any connection with the day already begun or that death could arrive this same afternoon, this afternoon which is so certain and which has every hour filled in advance.

Marcel Proust

I try never to miss an opportunity to sleep on my screened porch, going to sleep listening to the owls and all the other night sounds, and waking up to the sunrise and the fresh morning air.

Bill McEwen

True North

When it comes time to die, make sure all you've got to do is die.

Jim Elliot

It's easy to think external stimuli are the problem. But noises are just noises, sights are just sights, smart phones are just smart phones. We don't just react to things outside of us; we ourselves are continually creating distractions. We cook them up and keep them going. They are our companions, our pets. What lies behind these endless distractions is the boundless space of awakened mind.

Judy Lief

I have begun to look at my cancer surgeries as a great gift. A door seems to have opened to living with less certainty, greater intensity, and far more gratitude. Fear of the cancer's return, future surgery/treatment, pain, and dying bring an enduring sharpness. Even if my mortality might be imminent (and I hope it isn't!), I'm overwhelmed with gratitude for everything that comes my way. Dare I say it but this disease has made me feel more alive.

Bill McEwen

True North

What's here has its own life. What's here is it. We don't have to hurry through the now. Now is not the way to something else.

John Tarrant

Hopefully, at the end of my life I will leave something behind that will benefit future generations.

Bill McEwen

October 2014 will be my 26th year of making the trip North with my dogs and a friend. We're hunting wild birds, actually the "king of game birds", on public lands. Nothing is planted and nothing is guaranteed. October is a great time to be in the Northwoods, spending time with good friends, the challenge of getting a grouse or two, and watching the dogs work. I'm very fortunate to have had that opportunity.

Bill McEwen

I have never seen any proof that spiritually is connected to organized religion.

Bill McEwen

True North

How may I become increasingly present in such a way as to leave a trail for others who also intend to show up in their life experience?

Michael Brown

The time to make up your mind about other people is never.

From "The Philadelphia Story"

It often takes more guts to be gentle than it does to be confrontational.

George Saunders

The modalities of awakened doing are ACCEPTANCE, ENJOYMENT, and ENTHUSIASM.

Eckhart Tolle

To the mind that is still, the universe surrenders.

Lao Tzu

True North

True silence is becoming a unique experience; the patience to stand the silence is what separates a good turkey from a great turkey hunter.

Bill McEwen

Over the years the following two concepts have served me well: "If you can do anything to change your circumstances, why worry about it? If you cannot do anything to change your circumstances, why worry about it"? This is relevant to all situations in life and a great way to maintain balance.

Bill McEwen

Relationships are primary; tasks are secondary. What we do flows out of who we are.

Cornerstone Development

The name that can be told is not the eternal Tao. The name that can be named is not the eternal Name... Free from desire, you realize the mystery. Caught in desire, you only see the manifestations.

Tao Te Ching

True North

When you feel bad, let it be your link to other's suffering.
When you feel good, let it be your link to other's joy.

Pema Chodron

Religions are different roads converging to the same
point...if a man reaches the heart of his own religion; he
has reached the heart of others too.

Mahatma Gandhi

I have found that when I give my full attention to
something, that when I'm aligned with universal
intelligence, and doing something for the right reasons
(check my intention!), things just seem to flow, and I'm
always given the direction and guidance.

Bill McEwen

We are always hung up on our self serving notions- what I
want, what I need, what I like, what I think, what is best,
what is right- and that's the cause of suffering. We attach to
those ideas as though they were life itself. The truth is
never the phony things that we attach to in our heads. The
truth is as it is.

Karen Maezen Miller

True North

Everything could be taken from a person except for their ability to continue to hope- indeed their ability to CHOOSE to hope.

Viktor Frankl

The Buddha taught what he called the Four Noble Truths:

1. Life is suffering. Things change.
2. The origin of suffering is attachment. It hurts when things change.
3. The cessation of suffering is attainable. Accept that things change.
4. There is a way out of suffering. By changing yourself.

Karen Maezen Miller

When you confront any situation or problem, or anything you want to move forward, please think first about your intention. If your intention is to benefit only yourself, broaden it to help at least one other sentient being.

Dzigar Kongtrul Rinpoche

Each life-and within each life, each moment- has a meaning that is all its own.

Viktor Frankl

True North

This is the time. This is the place. This is the vastness. Right here is paradise. Always. Always.

Byron Katie

Turkey hunting is a series of instant tactical decisions that are invariably irreversible.

Tom Kelly

Properly trained, a man can be a dog's best friend.

Corey Ford

In every moment there is potential for something new. In every moment there is room for emergence. That's the miracle of evolution.

Andrew Cohen

We are adopting a mechanistic attitude toward life in which we believe that science has all the answers, and are abandoning the ancient verities and an appreciation of intangible values. We are confusing mores with morals.

Sigurd Olson

True North

Wherever my travels may lead, paradise is where I am.

Voltaire

A man tracks himself through life. One should be always on the trail of one's deepest nature, because it is the fearless living out of your own essential nature that connects you with the Divine.

Thoreau

A basic ecological truth which we still ignore is the interdependence and interaction of all living things, including man. This is the guiding principle guiding human destiny, and we know unless we choose wisely in the decades ahead, the fragile and intricate web of life could become a web of death.

Sigurd Olson

One cannot live the afternoon of life according to the program of life's morning, for what was great in the morning will be of little importance in the evening, and what in the morning was true will at evening have become a lie.

Carl Jung

True North

We are always trying hard to get somewhere. How would it feel just to stop all that effort and be still? We might be surprised at what happens!

Bill McEwen

There is much evidence on several levels that there are at least two major tasks to human life. The first task is to build a strong "container" or identity; the second is to find the contents that the container was meant to hold.

Richard Rohr

Spring comes with flowers, autumn with the moon. Summer comes with breezes and winter with snow. When useless concepts don't stick in your mind, THIS is your best season.

Wu-Men

Something happens to a man when he sits before a fire. Strange stirrings take place within him, and a light comes into his eye which was not there before. An open flame suddenly changes his environment to one of adventure and romance. Even an indoor fireplace has this effect though its owner is protected by four walls and the assurance that, should the fire go out, his thermostat will keep him warm. No matter where an open fire happens to be, in a city apartment, a primitive cabin, or deep in the wilderness, it weaves its spell.

Sigurd Olson

Under the full moon life is all adventure.

Sigurd Olson

I have realized that the past and future are real illusions that they exist in the present, which is what there is and all there is.

Alan Watts

When it's time for a new story to emerge, holding on to the past only intensifies our dilemma.

Bill McEwen

It seems to me that all significant change results from a change in meaning. Nothing changes until we interpret things differently. Change occurs when we let go of our certainty of our current views and develop a new understanding of what's going on.

Bill McEwen

Without a contemplative mind, we do not know how to hold creative tensions. We are better at rushing to judgment and demanding a complete resolution to things before we have learned what they have to teach us.

Richard Rohr

Peace has nothing to do with where you are and everything to do with how you SEE where you are.

Bill McEwen

When you live in a simple environment, your mind can become uncomplicated.

Ajahn Chah

We're all going to die, but it seems to me that many of us live each day as if it weren't so.

Bill McEwen

True North

Life has taught me that pain times resistance equals suffering.

Bill McEwen

Sooner or later if you are on any classic "spiritual schedule," some event, person, death, idea, or relationship will enter your life that you simply cannot deal with using your present skill set, your acquired knowledge, or your strong willpower. Spiritually speaking, you will be, you must be, led to the edge of your own private resources.

Richard Rohr

I have found over and over again that the places that I run away from are the places which need my attention. So, what are you running away from?

Bill McEwen

In spite of all similarities, every situation has, like a newborn child, a new face, that has never been before and will never come again. It demands of you a reaction that cannot be prepared beforehand. It demands nothing of what is past. It demands presence, responsibility; it demands you.

Martin Buber

The hard stuff is moderately easy. The soft stuff is incredibly hard. Without the soft stuff the hard stuff is meaningless.

Margaret Wheatley

You cannot continuously improve interdependent systems and processes unless you also work to perfect interdependent interpersonal relationships. Everything is connected!

Bill McEwen

Perhaps the most serious obstacle impeding the evolution of a land ethic is the fact that our educational and economic system is headed away from, rather than toward, an intense consciousness of land.

Aldo Leopold

True North

The more high-tech we become, the more nature we need to achieve NATURAL BALANCE. The mind/body/nature connection will enhance physical and mental health.

Richard Louv

The quiet and slowness of QiGong provide a chance to see ourselves clearly and objectively- our attributes and our flaws, both physical and mental- and gain the composure and resourcefulness to work with that raw material. We can learn patience, tolerance, and compassion for ourselves, and then turn those qualities outward toward other people and the planet. QiGong brings a force of balance to an out-of-balance world. It's a ritual that connects us with ourselves and with nature. In the end, I suppose that I do QiGong in order to become a better person.

Bill McEwen

The Buddha taught to lay down those things that lack a real abiding essence. If you lay those things down, you will see the truth. If you don't, you won't. That's the way it is. And when wisdom awakens within you, you will see the truth wherever you look. Truth is all you'll see.

Ajahn Chah

True North

This meditation business is potent stuff. Mindfulness meditation has been around for more than 2500 years, and I'm sure grateful for having stumbled on it. As a veteran magazine editor who spent 24/7 alert to trends, to the waves that move us, that make masses of us hunger for this and not that, I have no doubt that mindfulness meditation is an idea whose time has come- again.

Amy Gross

If you realize that all things change, there is nothing that you will try to hold on to. If you aren't afraid of dying, there is nothing that you can't achieve. Trying to control the future is like trying to take the master carpenter's tools; chances are that you'll cut your hand.

Tao Te Ching

We reached the old wolf in time to watch a fierce green fire dying in her eyes...I was young then and full of trigger itch; I thought that because fewer wolves meant more deer, that no wolves would mean hunter's paradise. But after seeing the green fire die, I sensed that neither the wolf nor the mountain agreed with such a view.

Aldo Leopold

True North

I have come to the conclusion that there are two educations: one that teaches how to make a living and one that teaches how to make a life. In my sessions and seminars, I focus on the latter.

Bill McEwen

The future was also where the bad stuff waited in ambush...now I know I can only control my tongue, my temper, and my appetite, but that's it. I have no effect on weather, traffic, or luck. I can't make good things happen. I can't know what will happen tomorrow, and I can't fix the past. What a relief.

Abigail Thomas

What passes for morality or spirituality in the vast majority of people's lives is the way everybody they grew up with thinks. Some would call it "conditioning" or even "scripting". Without very real inner work, most folks never get beyond it. It takes a huge push, much self doubt, and some degree of separation for people to find their own soul and their own destiny apart from what Mom and Dad always wanted them to be and do.

Richard Rohr

All that is worthwhile is action.

Teilhard de Chardin

True North

One of my biggest lessons in training dogs is the following: before I punish the dog, make certain that I'm not the cause of the offense.

Bill McEwen

Conservation, viewed in its entirety, is the slow and laborious unfolding of a new relationship between people and the land.

Aldo Leopold

Everyone has at least one true place, a piece of land or water that calls to them. Some of us search for such a place and call it home; and some of us finally come home. Where is your place?

Bill McEwen

After my cancer surgery and hospital stay and on returning home from Louisville, some words from one of John Denver's song kept playing in my head: "this ole farm feels like a long lost friend; hey it's good to be back home again."

Bill McEwen

True North

By non-doing, all doing becomes possible.

Lao Tzu

Throughout this book, as well as my first book, the word "change" occurs quite often. The fact that everything changes was recently reinforced very suddenly and without warning. A trip to Birmingham to visit my daughter and her family- intended to be another positive upside in a fruitful and comfortable existence- was turned upside down very quickly. One of their large golden retrievers running full force cut me down from behind and broke my ankle. Now several days after surgery, I realize that this is a great opportunity to practice and come to terms with these unexpected changes which happen in all our lives. I think the lesson here for all of us is that as we come to terms with these things we're becoming more prepared to really enjoy and appreciate life's easier moments, but also to be more present and at ease when things don't happen as we want them to, when others are facing illness, trouble, and death and when we are facing them ourselves. Internalizing and fully accepting uncertainty is a great spiritual practice.

Bill McEwen

True North

I have learned that happiness and unhappiness are in the way we meet the events in our lives and not in the nature of the events themselves.

Bill McEwen

In my new "handicapped" status words from another John Denver song popped into my mind:" some days are diamonds, some days are stones…sometimes the hard times won't leave me alone. Sometimes a cold wind blows a chill in my bones…some days are diamonds some days are stones". Whether my day is a "diamond" or a "stone", is all about choice.

Bill McEwen

In protecting this farm and this land with a conservation easement, what better gift of nature and "place" could I pass on to future generations?

Bill McEwen

Humans are a very small part of the cosmos. If you let humans get in the way of what is natural, you oppose yourself to the entirety of the universe. This takes a great deal of work: control of nature requires constant effort and in the long view (which is the only view the universe entertains, an eye blink or a billion years), it is doomed to fail.

Robert Rosenbaum

Life is so astonishing; it leaves very little time for anything else.

Emily Dickinson

Mindfulness is not about stress reduction or taking deep breaths. It is not a religion. It's a methodology that trains a capacity of your mind that generally receives little or no training…when the mind is trained to direct its full attention to whom and what we are encountering in this moment and when our mind is trained to be fully attentive, even in the midst of chaos, we have the space to make more wise and conscious choices.

Janice Marturano

I have found that mind training requires commitment, repetition, and lots of patience.

Bill McEwen

Somebody can put us in jail, but the only one who can take away our freedom is ourselves. When we give our responsibility for our suffering away to others, we are giving up our power to overcome the suffering.

Bill McEwen

Within the infinite depths of silence, words are irrelevant. However, if words are called for, they emerge out of the intelligence activated in the emptiness of inner peace.

Larry Rosenberg

The big secret of meditation, at least in the beginning stages, is that it gets you to a state where your mind is alert and relaxed at the same time. Happiness, then, is in the default state of mind: relaxed and clear at the same time…to me the biggest joke is that after all has been done in the history of the world in the pursuit of happiness, it turns out that sustainable happiness is achievable by simply bringing ones attention to ones breath. Life is funny. At least my life is.

Chade - Meng Tan

You are not what others think of you. Thoughts label but do not live. You cannot be summarized in a paragraph, or a song, much less captured in a name.

Bill McEwen

True North

No matter what time it is, it is always just now. Each moment is a moment of eternal time. A moment missed is a moment unlived.

Bill McEwen

Most game thinks that every man is a tall stump, but turkeys think that every tall stump is a man.

William Hanenkrat

There is nothing mysterious about meditation. It's really just mental training.

Chade- Meng Tan

Meditation is not something that is different from one's life…you should see your life and your meditation practice as one seamless thing. There should be no gap between formal practice and daily life.

Bill McEwen

Silence or engaged stillness is our great untapped resource. Without it, you're not living anywhere close to your full potential. But as your meditation practice continues, more and more your life emanates from this place of clear awareness. When seeing gets very clear and still, it is because "you" disappear. The great Chinese poet Li Po expressed this beautifully:"The birds have vanished down the sky. Now the last cloud drains away. We sit together, the mountain and me, until only the mountain remains".

Larry Rosenberg

To live is to be in relationship.

Vimila Thakar

Can we be with each other without the influence of old images, even though we have collected images of ourselves and each other over a whole life time? Are we aware of how these images color and distort our perceptions of each other? If we clearly understand this, can we carefully-caringly- look again as for the first time? Can we newly discover what is actually going on in this instant and respond from clarity rather than from ideas?

Toni Packer

You and I are not opposed to one another. Life is not necessarily a zero-sum game where if you have more then I'll have less. This is a fiction based on a narrow vision that pits self and others against one another. In reality we are all in this together.

Robert Rosenbaum

Several years ago and at the conclusion of a seminar, I was given a "homework assignment" which really hit home: "pay attention to how you are ACTUALLY living your life. Not how religious teachings tell you how you should live. Not how your parents or any of your scripting told you how to live. But how are you ACTUALLY living?"

Bill McEwen

The soul is like an acorn. Just as the acorn gives instruction to the oak about how to grow and what to become, the human soul- a type of spiritual blueprint- carries an image or vision that shows us how to grow, what gift we carry for others, and the nature of our true life. Unlike oaks, however, we humans are the one part of nature capable of ignoring or refusing the flowering of our own souls.

Bill Plotkin

One of the many lessons that my January 2013 cancer surgery taught me is that certain experiences cut us off entirely from nature, or at least that was my impression. As long as we inhabit bodies of flesh, blood, and bones, we are wholly inside and connected with nature. However, under medical duress, I think that we sometimes forget this. Flesh, blood, and bone notwithstanding, a body hooked up by way of tubes to suction devices, by way of an IV to a feeding tube or a synthetic morphine pump, has a tendency to forget its organic self. This experience taught me to be aware of something more than and probably worse than death: an existence dependent upon technology, machines, sterile procedures, hoses, pumps, chemicals easing one kind of pain only to feed a kind of psychic other. It seems to me that this is the way many people spend their last days alive; it's not a pleasant thought!

Bill McEwen

Self actualizing people, those who are psychologically and spiritually healthiest, are without one single exception, involved in a cause outside their own skins, and in something outside of themselves. They are devoted, working at something which is very precious to them- some calling or vocation in the old sense, the priestly sense. They are working at something which fate has called them to somehow and which they work at and which they love, so that the work-joy dichotomy in them disappears.

Abraham Maslow

If you are fully in the present moment, you are practicing, whether sitting in the bathroom or in a mountaintop hut.

True North

The present moment has immense significance. It's inexhaustible.

Larry Rosenberg

When people come here to stay at the "cabin" or to participate in a class or seminar, one of the things that I try to do is to help them to pause. And sometimes in pausing, a new frame of reference or a new perspective emerges.

Bill McEwen

What truth are you hiding from? Right now.

Josh Baran

Every hunt and walk in the Northwoods is different and each presents a discovery of some sort, big or small. When you grouse hunt, you don't just move through the woods as a hiker might; you interact with it. It harbors clues for success: a ripe thorn apple thicket, drumming in the distance, a "just right" aspen grove, clover and "droppings" on the trail, and so many other clues. Keep quieter than quiet and the woods will monitor your hunt!

Bill McEwen

True North

I slept and dreamt that life was joy; I awoke and saw that life was service; I acted and behold, service.

Tagore

We spend so much of our time caught up in memories of the past or looking ahead to the future, full of worries and plans. The breath has none of that "other timeness". When we observe the breath, we are automatically placed in the present. A mindful observation of such a miniature model of life itself leads to insights that are broadly applicable to the rest of our experience.

Henepola Gunaratauna

Facing my own mortality in a death-phobic culture can often be a lonely process. However, in wild places like the Northwoods around Lake Superior or in the woods and hills surrounding my home, things are quite different. The evidence is everywhere and tells me that I am not alone: in the skull of an immature eagle I found on the lake shore; in the bones of a deer in the field behind my house; in the corpse of a coyote in the dry creek bed; in the fall of a maple leaf from its branch. All these things tell me that death is true, right, graceful; not tragic, not failure, not defeat.

Bill McEwen

True North

I am learning (by trial and error!) that what matters most is the quality of mind that I bring to whatever it is that I'm doing.

Bill McEwen

I have found that people go to the wilderness for many things, but the most important of these is perspective. They may think that they go for fishing, hunting, the scenery, or companionship, but in reality it is for something much deeper. They go to the wilderness for the good of their souls.

Sigurd Olson

It has been said and from my own observation, I would agree, that 90% of people seem to be living 90% of their lives on cruise control, which in essence is to be asleep or unconscious.

Bill McEwen

True North

Once you create a self-justifying story line, your emotional entrapment within it quadruples.

Pema Chodron

It's hard to place a price tag on these things, on the sights, sounds, and smells and memories of the out-of- doors, on the countless things that we have seen and loved. They are the dividends of a good life.

Sigurd Olson

Persona and shadow are correlative terms- your shadow is what you refuse to see about yourself, and what you do not want others to see. The more you have cultivated and protected a chosen persona, the more shadow work you will need to do. Be especially careful, therefore, of any idealized role or self image like that of minister, mother, doctor, nice person, professor, moral believer, or president of this or that.

Richard Rohr

True North

There are known knowns; there are things we know we know. We also know there are known unknowns; that is to say we know there are some things we do not know. But there are also unknown unknowns- the ones we don't know we don't know.

Donald Rumsfeld

Three rules of work: out of clutter find simplicity; from discord find harmony; in the middle of difficulty lies opportunity.

Albert Einstein

In Chinese medicine, it is the heart that plays key roles in regulating our emotions, and hence, our health.

Bill McEwen

The power of consciousness cannot be overstated. Where we put our consciousness, we put our life energy.

Bill McEwen

True North

It is only possible to live happily- ever- after on a day- to-day basis.

Margaret Bonnano

We have no dominion over what the world will do to us, all of us. What the earth will make of our tinkering and abuse can be modeled by computers but is, in the end, beyond our reckoning, our science. Nature is simply not done to. Nature talks back. Nature responds. Nature is willful.

Eva Saulitis

The power of a movement lies less in attacking an enemy's untruth than in naming and claiming a truth of one's own. The decision to live "divided no more" is less a strategy for changing other people's lives than an expression of the elemental need for one's own core values to come to the fore.

Parker Palmer

True North

In nature, death is not a defeat; but that's a hard comfort as we all face our own. Can I take comfort in the countless births and deaths this earth enacts each moment?

Eva Saulitis

As a society we are increasingly concerned about air pollution, water pollution, electronic pollution, and noise pollution, but how mindful are we about the pollution caused by our own unconsciousness?

Robert Peng

Leading a spiritual life in the secular world can be a real challenge and requires great strength of character. There is a saying: "the lesser sage lives in the mountains while the greater sage lives in the city".

Bill McEwen

I have prayed for years for one good humiliation a day. And then I must watch my reaction to it.

Richard Rohr

True North

Standing on the bank of the Brule River with no sound except the rippling water, watching an eagle soar against a cloudless sky, and feeling the cold wind on my face is a very spiritual experience.

Bill McEwen

Perhaps the poet William Blake said it best: "to see the world in a grain of sand and heaven in a wildflower; hold infinity in the palm of your hand and eternity in an hour".

Bill McEwen

Listen to your life; all moments are key moments.

Frederick Buechner

American higher education has one glaring deficiency. It does not teach undergraduates how to live. It teaches them when the French Revolution was, what the carbon cycle is, and how to solve for X. It does not tell them what to do when they feel confused, alone, and scared. When they breakdown after a breakup. When they are so depressed they cannot get out of bed or when they drink themselves into unconsciousness every night. When they turn to drugs for relief from their pain or when their divorced parents just won't stop fighting. When they're thinking about suicide or when they wonder about the meaning of it all. When they are terrified by the question: what do I do next?

Marshall Poe

One of the goals in the work I do is to get everyone to invest more in the most important asset we have in this nation- well functioning human beings, specifically teachers and students.

Bill McEwen

Listening is magic: it turns a person from an object outside, opaque or dimly threatening, to an intimate experience, and therefore into a friend. In this way, listening softens and transforms the listener.

Norman Fischer

True North

Mindfulness means paying attention in a particular way: on purpose, in the present moment, with complete acceptance, and non-judgmentally.

Jon Kabat-Zinn

This being human is a guest house, every morning a new arrival: a joy, a depression, a meanness, some momentary awareness comes as an unexpected visitor. Welcome them all! Even if they are a crowd of sorrows who violently sweep your house empty of its furniture, still, treat each guest honorably. He may be clearing you out for some future delight. The dark thought, the shame, the malice, meet them all at the door laughing, and invite them in. Be grateful for whoever comes, because each has been sent as a guide from beyond.

Rumi

Lewis and Clark were lost most of the time. If your idea of exploration is to always know where you are and to be inside your zone of competence, you don't do wild new shit. You have to be confused, upset, and think you're stupid. If you're not willing to do that, you can't go outside the box.

Nathan Myhrvold

True North

If the wisest sages of the pre-modern world were to suddenly materialize in contemporary society and spend a few days examining our achievements, they would most certainly marvel at our technological advances- our cars, our smart phones, our computers- but they would be equally perplexed by our blatant ignorance about our own Life Force.

Robert Peng

One of the biggest lessons I've learned in my exploration of Chinese medicine and in my Qigong practice is simply this: "where the mind goes, Qi follows."

Bill McEwen

I am a believer in regular body work: both Rolfing and massages have served me well. Although somewhat different in focus, each one helps to improve alignment, remove toxins from throughout the body, improve circulation, enhance bodily awareness, and reduce stress. Both are excellent modalities for integrating mind, body, heart, and soul.

Bill McEwen

Everything is mind made.

Bill McEwen

True North

Our brains come from a time when we were adapted to natural settings, not urban settings.

Gregory Bratman

One of the great things about life is that sometimes memories happen without warning.

Bill McEwen

Sir William Osler made the following statement: "it is more important to know what type of person has a disease than what disease a person has". Perhaps in the future decades, our medical profession will continue to move toward a more holistic and integrative paradigm. This is one of the big lessons that Traditional Chinese Medicine has to offer.

Bill McEwen

It is not how much you do, but how much love you put into the doing that matters.

Mother Teresa

True North

The most precious gift that we can offer others is our presence. When mindfulness embraces those we love, they will bloom like flowers.

Thich Nhat Hanh

If you can remember only one thing that I've said about breathing and the breath, let it be the following: "breathe as if your life depended on it!"

Bill McEwen

If you are distressed by anything external, the pain is not due to the thing itself, but to your estimate of it; and this you have the power to revoke at any moment.

Marcus Aurelius

The outer world is necessary for the inner world; they are not two worlds but rather a single world with two aspects: the outer and the inner. If we don't have certain outer experiences, we don't have certain inner experiences, or at least don't have them in a profound way. We need the sun, the stars, the rivers, the moon, the mountains and birds, the fish in the sea to evoke a world of mystery, to evoke the sacred. It gives us a sense of awe. This is a response to the cosmic liturgy, since the universe itself is a sacred liturgy.

Thomas Berry

When you tug on a string in nature, you find it connected to everything else.

John Muir

What would life be like if we were as immersed in nature as we are in all our technology? This is a question that I find myself asking on a regular basis. I think that, perhaps, we might be happier, healthier, experience fewer cases of depression, anxiety, and attention deficit disorder. I also suspect that violence would decrease and that we would begin to build more sustainable communities and healthier families.

Bill McEwen

True North

If you clearly see the truth through meditation then suffering will become UNWOUND, just like a screw. When you unwind a screw, it withdraws. It's not tightly fixed as when you screw it, clockwise. The mind withdraws like this. It lets go, it relinquishes. It's not tightly bound within good and evil, within possessions, praise and blame, happiness and suffering. If we don't know the truth, it's like tightening the screw all the time. You screw it down until it crushes you, and you suffer over everything. When you UNWIND out of all of that, you become free and at peace.

Ajahn Chah

We need the tonic of the wilderness.

Henry David Thoreau

If there is an underlying theme or guideline in all my sessions it would be the following: "let's have fun, keep it simple, stick to the present moment, and be open to whatever arises."

Bill McEwen

True North

The breeze at dawn has secrets to tell you. Don't go back to sleep. You must ask for what you really want. Don't go back to sleep. People are going back and forth across the door sill where the two worlds touch. The door is round and open. Don't go back to sleep.

Rumi

...the key active ingredient in the formula for world peace may be something as simple as meditation. It's such a simple solution to such an intractable problem. It's almost absurd. Except that it may actually work...But how? How does one make the benefits of meditation accessible to humanity? The answer to that question is something I call the Three Easy Steps to World Peace: start with me; make meditation a field of science; align meditation with life.

Chade-Meng Tan

Thousands of tired, nerve-shaken, over civilized people are beginning to find out that going to the mountains is going home; that wilderness is a necessity; and that mountain parks and reservations are useful not only as fountains of timber and irrigating rivers, but as fountains of life.

John Muir

True North

Perhaps the best preparation for the remainder of the 21st century and beyond may be a combination of natural and virtual experience. In this way we might be able to combine the knowledge and powers of our ancestors with the digital speed of our teenagers.

Bill McEwen

What do the Arab's think about American attempts to "promote democracy?" A stunning 3 percent believe these efforts made a difference. If you ask people in Iraq, I think it is about 1 percent.

Norm Chomsky

Sometimes I wonder whether the world is being run by smart people who are putting us on or by imbecibles who really mean it.

Mark Twain

What if the great work of the 21st century turned out to be, not our obsession with all our "gadgets", but rather a reconnection with the natural world as a source of meaning?

Bill McEwen

I do not want the peace which passes understanding. I want the peace which brings understanding.

Helen Keller

The most effective paths to soul are nature based. Nature- the outer nature we call "the wild"- has always been the essential element and the primary setting for the journey to the soul. The soul, after all, is our "inner" wilderness, the intrapsychic terrain we know the least and that holds our individual mysteries.

Bill Plotkin

If science cannot lead us to wisdom as well as power, it is surly no science at all.

Aldo Leopold

True North

You can't teach what you don't possess.

John Wooden

A new idea is, of course, never created by one idea alone. A prophet is one who recognizes the birth of an idea in the collective mind, and who defines and clarifies, with his life, its meanings and implications.

Aldo Leopold

The greatest capacity of humans, the one that distinguishes us from other species, is our consciousness and the awareness that we always have a choice. I have come to the conclusion that choice trumps genetics. For example, I may or may not have a genetic predisposition to consume alcohol or some other drug, but in the final analysis, I will always have a choice.

Bill McEwen

True North

The secret of the Tao is found in the smallest detail of the ordinary day.

Lao Tzu

Here's a homework assignment for you: go and explore one of your "ordinary" days without a story line or any preconceived ideas and look at everything as if you are seeing it for the first time.

Bill McEwen

Our power to disorganize the land is growing faster than our understanding of it, or our affection for it.

Aldo Leopold

There are two spiritual dangers in not owning a farm. One is the danger that supposes that breakfast comes from the grocery and the other is that heat comes from the furnace.

Aldo Leopold

True North

The essence of our practice is to watch intention and examine the mind. You must have wisdom. Don't discriminate. Don't get upset with others if they are different. Would you get upset with a small and crooked tree in the forest for not being tall and straight like some of the others? That would be silly. Don't judge other people. There are all varieties. There's no need to carry the burden of wishing to change them all. If you want to change anything, change your ignorance to wisdom.

Ajahn Chah

Wisdom seeing has always sought to change the seer first, and then knows what is seen will largely take care of itself. It is almost that simple, and it is always that hard.

Richard Rohr

We cannot put off living until we are ready. The most significant characteristic of life is its urgency, "here and now" without any possible postponement. Life is fired at us point blank.

Jose Ortega y Gasset

True North

Every emotional experience that we have is not just psychological; our physical bodies are also affected. It is also a physiological experience.

Bill McEwen

Emotional intelligence is trainable, even in adults. This claim is based on a fairly new branch of science known as "neuroplasicity". This is the idea that what we think, do, and pay attention to changes the structure and function of our brains. So how do we begin training emotional intelligence? We begin by training ATTENTION.

Chade –Meng Tan

Should the time ever come when we allow our engrossment with comfort and technological progress to erase our longings to the point where we no longer dream of an unspoiled world, then I fear for America.

Sigurd Olson

True North

It is the mark of an educated mind to be able to entertain a thought without accepting it.

Aristotle

Distractedness is one sign that we are avoiding the truth of the moment. A mindful inquiry- What is keeping me from being in the present? - can aid that subtle attunement. Sometimes the answer reveals the hidden influence of our most deeply engrained emotional patterns.

Tara Bennett-Goleman

In 2005, in "Last Child in the Woods" I introduced the term NATURE DEFICIT DOSORDER, not as a medical diagnosis, but as a way to describe the growing gap between children and nature. After the book's publication, I heard many adults speak with heartfelt emotion, even anger, about this separation, but also about their own sense of loss…every day, our relationship with nature, or the lack of it, influences our lives. This has always been true. But in the 21st century our survival- or thrival- will require a transformative framework for that relationship, a reunion of humans with the rest of nature.

Richard Louv

True North

In dealing with many different organizations over the years, one of my key insights has been: "if you understand the people and you understand the interactions between them, you will understand the whole organization."

Bill McEwen

The mind is stubborn as a horse and as hard to train. What do you do when you've got a horse that's stubborn? Don't feed it for awhile and it will soon come around again. And when it listens to your command, feed it a little. We can train the mind in the same way. With right effort, wisdom will arise.

Ajahn Chah

The world can appear very convincing. Don't be deceived. Although what we see, hear, and feel is reality, at best it is a small window; at worst it is a distorting filter. All of our perceptions are colored and filtered by our senses and the

True North

language we use to get a handle on our ungraspable experience.

Robert Rosenbaum

In any situation it's very hard to act skillfully unless we see the situation clearly and have the right intention.

Bill McEwen

The real enemies of our life are the "oughts" and the "ifs". They pull us back into the unalterable past and forward into the unpredictable future. But real life takes place in the here and now. God is a God of the present. God is always in the moment, be that moment hard or easy, joyful or painful.

Henry Nouwen

To me the smell of balsam in the Northwoods is very special and is usually an indication of good grouse habitat. It's a fragrance that I can never quite forget and can never quite remember.

Bill McEwen

True North

There is a certain joy and satisfaction in finding and naming your own trails and grouse coverts: the long trail; the honey hole; Boyce's trail; lone pine. You hope that no other grouse hunter ever goes there, and I suppose that it's possible to trick yourself into believing that no one ever does!

Bill McEwen

If you hunt ruffed grouse long enough in the Northwoods, you'll eventually begin to yearn for the country as much as for the birds.

Bill McEwen

Every species of beast and bird, of reptile and sea creature, can be tamed and has been tamed by the human species, but no one can tame the tongue- a restless evil full of deadly poison.

James 3:7, 8

True North

The only way to achieve maximum openness is to arrive at every moment without any preconception. Otherwise, we resist what doesn't fit our model. Regardless of how much we know or how evolved we have become, we must put every bit of that aside. We must step in the mystery naked and undefended.

Raphael Cushnir

The lesson which life repeats and constantly enforces is "pay attention", "learn quickly", "look under foot", and "everything is a teacher". Having to be on crutches for six weeks with my broken ankle has afforded me a great opportunity to "revisit" all of the above. In addition and upon reflection, the words "mindfulness", "patience", "acceptance", and "compassion" all come to mind. What a great opportunity to deepen my practice…and to finish this book!

Bill McEwen

One of the things I enjoy most about ruffed grouse hunting is that nature and I are on the same plane…and more often than not, nature has the upper hand!

Bill McEwen

True North

Each year these contracts with game animals (the birds!) are renewed, rewritten. Each year you grow older, and there are new terms.

Barry Lopez

One knows a landscape not by knowing the name or identity of everything in it but by perceiving and experiencing everything in it.

Barry Lopez

What you do not see, do not hear, do not experience, you will never really know.

Alaska Eskimo Elder

You search for God through heaven and earth but you don't know the one who is right before your eyes because you don't know to search into this very moment.

Jesus

True North

I have learned over the years that one of the things that I share with all living beings is that we all have a tendency to repeat what we find pleasurable and shrink from what gives us pain. What a fertile field for exploration and to work at holding the "creative tension" between the two.

Bill McEwen

Express yourself completely, and then keep quiet. Be like the forces of nature: when it rains, there is only rain; when it blows, there is only wind; when the clouds pass, the sun shines through. Open yourself to the Tao, and then trust your actual responses. Then everything will fall into place.

Tao Te Ching

The animal body for all its susceptibility and vertigo remains the primary instrument of all our knowing, as the capricious earth remains our primary cosmos.

David Abram

True North

True insight has no thinking in it. It is a DIRECT
EXPERIENCE that becomes bone deep with no separation
between what you know and who you are.

Bill McEwen

...whether or not you notice its active influence, it is the
mountain that defines the mood of this moment where you
stand. To step into the shadow of this mountain is to step
directly under the mountain's influence letting it untangle
your senses as the rhythm of your breath adjusts its
breathing, to the style of its weather. To step into the
shadow is to become a part, if only for this moment, of the
mountain's life.

David Abram

The volume of information at our disposal is, in fact,
leading to less rather than more certainty. The number of
voices and opinions we can hear on any given issue is so
dauntingly large that we often don't know who or what to
believe or follow.

Janice Marturano

True North

The transformation of suffering that comes out of awareness is most powerful when it is and has been intimate with the experience of my own life. Only then does it become "real".

Bill McEwen

A change of feeling is a change of destiny.

Neville

He who stands on tiptoe doesn't stand firm. He who rushes ahead doesn't go far. He who tries to shine dims his own light. He who defines himself can't know who he really is. He who has power over others can't empower himself. He who clings to his work will create nothing that endures. If you want to accord with the Tao, just do your job, then let go.

Tao Te Ching

True North

When I'm fully aware of my resistance to anything, there also emerges a great opportunity for wisdom to develop by noticing what is actually happening.

Bill McEwen

Awareness is never limited to a particular time, place, or posture; and neither is the breath. If you're not breathing, you're dead. Mindfulness, the breath, and movement are all happening within the same time frame. Can you be simple and alert enough to know this unitary event as it is? I feel much more alive and in "tune" when my body and breath are permeated with the energy of awareness.

Bill McEwen

Whoever you are, no matter how lonely, the world offers itself to you.

Mary Oliver

Many of our inherited concepts (our ready definitions and explanations) serve to isolate our intelligence from its intimacy from our creaturely encounter with the strangeness of things.

David Abram

A clear mind is a form of nonconceptual intelligence that can respond wisely to a given situation, at the moment it arises.

Bill McEwen

Neuroscience is now showing us that the mind's capacity for multitasking is extremely limited. We're really built for doing one thing at a time.

Janice Marturano

With even a little intuitive wisdom we will be able to see clearly through the ways of the world. We will come to understand that everything in the world is a teacher. Trees and vines, for example, can reveal the nature of reality to us. With wisdom, there is no need to question anyone, no need to study. We can learn enough from nature to be enlightened.

Ajahn Chah

True North

How sad if we pass through life and never see it with the eyes of a child.

Bill McEwen

Our goal should be to live life in radical amazement, to look at the world in a way that takes nothing for granted. Everything is phenomenal, everything is incredible; to be spiritual is to be constantly amazed.

Abraham Joshua Heschel

I do not know whether it is possible to love the planet or not, but I do know that it is possible to love the places we can see, touch, smell, and experience.

David Orr

You can't know who you are until you know where you are.

Wendell Berry

True North

Every solid thing, whether a toothpick or a trumpet, a porcelain plate or helicopter, is fashioned from materials once birthed by the earth.

David Abram

Do not believe what you have heard. Do not believe in tradition because it is handed down many generations. Do not believe in anything that has been spoken of many times. Do not believe because the written statements come from some old sage. Do not believe in conjecture. Do not believe in authority or teachers or elders. But after careful observation and analysis, when it agrees with reason and it will benefit one and all, then accept it and live by it.

The Buddha

There is a fundamental difference between knowing something and knowing about something. "Knowing about" is another term for belief. "Knowing" is a term reserved exclusively for direct experience, which means an absence of doubt. You cannot learn anything through the efforts of others. The world's greatest teachers can teach you absolutely nothing unless you are willing to apply what they have to offer based on your knowing.

Bill McEwen

Have you ever had an original thought? I was asked that question recently and have been thinking about it ever since. I really don't think that I have…quite a revelation!

Bill McEwen

There is a law in psychology that if you form a picture in your mind of what you would like to be, and if you keep and hold that picture long enough, you will soon become exactly as you have been thinking.

William James

The mental creation precedes the physical creation.

Stephen Covey

True North

Here's the truth: sometimes the game plays you. You labor into a headwind and suddenly the wind shifts and it's at your back...none of us has a perfect life, nor are we in command even of our own bodies; we borrow, we don't own.

Pat Summitt

Here's another question for you to ponder: if your past were taken away and completely erased from your memory, who or what would you be?

Bill McEwen

Except ye be converted and become as little children, ye shall not enter the Kingdom of Heaven.

Jesus

Men are disturbed not by things that happen, but by their opinions of the things that happen.

Epictetus

True North

Trying to end suffering without first understanding the cause is like pulling on a rope that's stuck. You just pull the end of the rope over here. The other end of the rope over there is still stuck over there so it never comes. What to do to make it come? It does not come free because you never seek out the source, the root. You just get lost on pulling on this end. What is it stuck on? It must be stuck on something, and that's why it doesn't come. Go to the source, untie the knot, and be free.

Ajahn Chah

I really haven't found any better way to develop insight except through a daily practice of quieting the mind, tuning in with all the senses, being patient and open to just sitting, and being willing to watch all my thoughts just come and go. As the world of insanity continues to escalate, I think it behooves all of us to do some form of mindfulness each day.

Bill McEwen

Nature is not a place to visit, it is home.

Gary Snyder

True North

The universe is full of magical things patiently waiting for our wits to grow sharper.

Eden Phillpotts

Men are born soft and supple; dead they are hard and stiff. Plants are born tender and pliant; dead, they are brittle and dry. Thus whoever is stiff and inflexible is a disciple of death. Whoever is soft and yielding is a disciple of life. The hard and stiff will be broken. The soft and supple will prevail.

Tao Te Ching

In most of my life experiences, relationships seem to hold the key to most everything. Technology may enable us to be efficient, but it cannot take the place of the human relationship. Technology, like the body, is a good servant but a bad master. From my perspective, high tech works in the long run only with high touch.

Bill McEwen

True North

When you are dead, seek for your resting place not in the earth, but in the hearts of men.

Rumi

We must become the change we seek in the world.

Gandhi

Patience is a key ingredient in the process of the natural world and in our personal world. For example, when I broke my ankle a month ago, the healing process is proceeding precisely at its own pace independent of any opinion I may have about it. My desire to have it mend quickly is of absolutely no consequence. If I were to become impatient, I might actually do something to prevent it from healing thoroughly. Shakespeare said it best: "How poor are they that have not patience! What wound did ever heal but by degree?"

Bill McEwen

True North

Many of us think that happiness is not possible in the present moment. Most of us believe that there are a few more conditions that need to be met before we can be happy. This is why we are sucked into the future and are not capable of being present in the here and now. That is why we step over the many wonders of life. If we keep running away into the future, we cannot be in touch with the many wonders of life-we cannot be in the present moment where there is healing, transformation, and joy.

Thich Nhat Hanh

When the infrastructure shifts, everything rumbles.

Stan Davis

From my life experience, communication is without question the most important skill in life. And probably the most important component of communication is LISTENING. I've learned far more in my life by listening than I have by talking!

Bill McEwen

True North

As soon as you rise above mere survival, the question of meaning and purpose becomes of paramount importance in your life. Many people feel caught up in the routines of daily living that seem to deprive their life of significance...but the true or primary purpose of your life cannot be found on the outer level. It does not concern what you do but who you are-that is to say, your state of consciousness...so the most important thing to realize is this: you life has an inner purpose and an outer purpose. Inner purpose concerns being and is primary. Outer purpose concerns doing and is secondary.

Eckhart Tolle

There is nothing as powerful as an idea whose time has come.

Victor Hugo

A man who gives in to temptation after five minutes simply does not know what it would have been like an hour later. That is why bad people, in a sense, know very little about badness. They have lived a sheltered life by always giving in.

C.S. Lewis

True North

My object in living is to unite my avocation and my vocation as my two eyes make one in sight. Only where love and need are one and the work is play for mortal stakes, is the deed ever really done for Heaven and future's sakes.

Robert Frost

Author Jones said the following: "all organizations are perfectly aligned to get the results they get." I would submit that the same holds true for individuals. If you don't like the results that you're presently getting in your life, then you need to consider carefully examining your view of reality. When was the last time that you honestly challenged some of your perceptions?

Bill McEwen

Wisdom denotes the pursuing of the best ends by the best means.

Frances Hutcheson

True North

I think that you must know yourself in order to know the world. The more you inhabit yourself, the more you'll find your home is not a matter of square footage, but rather a sense of residing wherever you find yourself: more resonance than residence. The more you feel at home in the world, the less you'll need to carry. With a lighter pack on your shoulders, it becomes easier to feel content; and when you are content, you feel at peace.

Bill McEwen

There is one thing that is common to every individual, relationship, team, family, organization, nation, economy, and civilization throughout the world-one thing if removed will destroy the most powerful government, the most successful business, the most thriving economy, the most influential leadership, the greatest friendship, the strongest character, the deepest love. On the other hand, if developed and leveraged, that one thing has the potential to create unparalleled success and prosperity in every dimension of life. Yet, it is the least understood, most neglected, and most underestimated possibility of our time. THAT ONE THING IS TRUST.

Stephen M.R. Covey

True North

Every time one of these high- level and deep- seeded incidents (scandals) is uncovered, the American public trusts a little bit less, and we just don't bounce back as fast.

Robert Eckert

One of the first lessons which I learned as a young Marine officer was very simple but yet very profound: moral authority always trumps formal authority. Who I was spoke much louder than my rank or position. I found out very quickly that by being personally trustworthy and by giving trust to those in my stewardship until they proved unworthy of that trust, we could get a lot more done and could accomplish our missions.

Bill McEwen

What upsets me is not that you lied to me, but that I can no longer believe you.

Friedrich Nietzsche

True North

What Gandhi thinks, what he feels, what he says, and what he does is all the same. He does not need notes…you and I, we think one thing, feel another, say a third, and do a fourth, so we need notes and a file to keep track.

Mahadev Desai

Technique and technology are important, but adding trust is the issue of the decade.

Tom Peters

What do we mean by "dead"? Who should declare if an individual is dead? A priest? A lawyer? A doctor? A machine? A noted neurologist and the Dali Lama recently discussed these issues at a conference in Brazil, and surprisingly, they both agreed strongly on one point: we need to create an ethical framework for science that is based on secular, rather than religious views; science alone should define what we mean by death.

Roger Highfield

We are cursed with the blessing of consciousness and choice, a two-edged sword that both divide us and can help us to become whole. But choosing wholeness, which sounds like a good thing, turns out to be a risky business, making us vulnerable in ways we would prefer to avoid.

Parker Palmer

Developing stronger emotional intelligence is one of the greatest challenges faced by parents and leaders at all levels of organizations.

Stephen Covey

The divided life is a wounded life and the soul keeps calling us to heal the wound. Ignore that call, and we find ourselves trying to numb our pain with an anesthetic of choice, be it substance abuse, overwork, consumerism, or mindless media noise. Such anesthetics are easy to come by in a society that wants to keep us divided and unaware of our pain- for the divided life that is pathological for individuals can serve social systems well, especially when it comes to those functions that are morally dubious.

Parker Palmer

True North

I have learned that there is no quick fix for the alienation from soul. Cultivating a relationship to soul and transforming your life take time and hard work. I think that your ego must be shocked or shifted in a way that extracts you from the surface of your life.

Bill McEwen

Whenever we touch any entity, we are also being touched by that entity.

David Abram

To believe in something and not live it is dishonest.

Gandhi

I only went out for a walk, and finally concluded to stay out until sundown, for going out, I found, was really going in.

John Muir

True North

Silence is the space in which one awakens, and the noisy mind is the space in which one remains asleep. If your mind continues chattering, you are asleep.

Osho

Your field of energy radiates at whatever vibratory frequency you generate. You are impacting and are being impacted by the energy fields of many people each day. Don't give your energy to things you don't want or don't believe in!

Bill McEwen

No man is an island, entire of itself; every man is a piece of the continent, a part of the main; if a clod be washed away by the sea, Europe is less, as well as is a promontory were, as well as if a manor of thy friends or thine own were; any man's death diminishes me, because I am involved in mankind; and therefore never send to know for whom the bell tolls; it tolls for thee.

John Donne

True North

Often it seems as if we are creating a society of mental giants and emotional infants. Both heart and mind have to be involved in this journey we call life. The mind understands, connects, and discerns, whereas the heart feels.

Bill McEwen

I find that there are many people so busy saying "yes" that there is no time left to say "no". It's no wonder that stress is running rampant in our culture!

Bill McEwen

Impermanence, unsatisfactoriness, and no self are the three characteristics to be found in all existence. We can only gain insight into these three things through personal experience. Nobody knows these unless they have seen them for themselves. They are very nice words, which most of you may be familiar with, but you need to realize them through direct inner knowledge. Although we experience them every single moment, we're usually not paying enough attention.

Ayya Khema

True North

Ninety percent of all leadership failures are character failures.

Stephen Covey

The ego could be defined simply in this way: a dysfunctional relationship with the present moment...there are three ways in which the ego will treat the present moment: as a means to an end, as an obstacle, or as an enemy.

Eckhart Tolle

In our way of life, our government, with every decision we make, we always keep in mind the seventh generation to come. It is our job to see the people coming ahead, the generations still unborn, have a world no worse than ours-hopefully better. When we walk upon Mother Earth we always plant our feet carefully because we know the faces of our future generations are looking up at us from beneath the ground. We never forget them.

Oren Lyons

True North

The county records may allege that you own this pasture, but the plover airily rules out such trivial legalities. He has just flown 4,000 miles to reassert the title he got from the Indians, and until the young plovers are a-wing, this pasture is his, and none may trespass without his protest.

Aldo Leopold

To honor and respect means to think of the land and the water and plants and animals that live here as having a right equal to our own to be here. We are not the supreme and all knowing beings living at the top of the pinnacle of evolution, but in fact we are members of the sacred hoop of life, along with trees and rocks, the coyotes and the eagles and fish and toads that each fulfills its purpose. They each perform their given task in the sacred hoop, and we have one, too.

Wolf Song

When you are going nowhere in particular and just marking time, there is nothing better than being knocked on your ass. Mindless mediocrity needs a hard right to the solar plexus. When you find yourself in a permanent holding pattern, getting hit from the blind side may well be the best thing that could happen.

Bill McEwen

A walk is one of the secrets of dodging old age. I recommend it to people who are growing old against their will. The forest awakens the same feeling it did when I was a boy. It is the old trees that have all the beauty and grandeur.

Ralph Waldo Emerson

It is a greater compliment to be trusted than to be loved.

George McDonald

At sunset on the last day of grouse season, every blackberry blows out its light. I cannot understand how a mere bush can thus be infallibly informed about the Wisconsin statutes, nor have I ever gone back the next day to find out. For the ensuing eleven months the lanterns glow only in recollection. I sometimes think that the other months were constituted mainly as a fitting interlude between Octobers, and I suspect that dogs and perhaps grouse, share the same view.

Aldo Leopold

A healthy lifestyle really doesn't cost a penny. All you have to do is CHOOSE it…easier said than done!

Bill McEwen

One of the next big breakthroughs in medicine, and we're beginning to see it now, is the patient taking responsibility for his or her health. What you eat, as well as what you do and how you conduct your life, can produce astonishing new levels of health and fitness.

Bill McEwen

Only when you act from the center is your act total. And when that act is total, it has a beauty of its own. When the act is total, it is moment to moment. When the act is total, you don't carry the memory- you need not.

Osho

True North

The history of free man is never written by chance but by choice-their choice.

Dwight Eisenhower

In a few hundred years, when the history of our time is written from a long term perspective, it is likely that the most important event those historians will see is not technology, not the Internet, not e-commerce. It is an unprecedented change in the human condition. For the first time- literally- substantial and rapidly growing numbers of people have choices. For the first time, they will have to manage themselves. And society is totally unprepared for it.

Peter Drucker

The significant problems we face cannot be solved at the same level of thinking we were at when we created them.

Einstein

True North

There is in our civilization a great deal of ignorance about the human condition, and the more spiritually ignorant you are, the more you suffer. Until now, human intelligence, which is no more than a minute aspect of intelligence, has been distorted and misused by the ego. I call that "intelligence in the service of madness."

Eckhart Tolle

As I watch the history of the world unfold here in the summer of 2014, the above quote really resonates with me. I remember my feelings when Khe Sanh was abandoned, when the last helicopter left Saigon, and when we withdrew from South Vietnam. This scenario is now repeating itself once again in the Middle East. Someone once said "Stupidity is relatively harmless, but intelligent stupidity is highly dangerous."

Bill McEwen

The primary factor in creation is consciousness, and our next evolutionary hurdle will be to manifest this new state. No matter how active we are, how much effort we make, our state of consciousness creates our world, and if there is no change on that inner level, no amount of action will make any difference. We will only re-create modified versions of the same world again and again.

Eckhart Tolle

Mistrust doubles the cost of doing business.

John Whitney

The range by what we think and do is limited by what we fail to notice. And because we fail to notice that we fail to notice, there is little we can do to change, until we notice how failing to notice shapes our thoughts and deeds.

R.D. Laing

Chesty Puller once said that the two most difficult things to accomplish as a Marine were the following: earning the gold bar of a second lieutenant; being promoted to brigadier general. I can vouch for the first but have no experience as to the second!

Bill McEwen

True North

I know this now. Every man gives his life to what he believes. Every woman gives her life for what she believes. Sometimes people believe in little or nothing, and so they give their lives to little or nothing...

Joan of Arc

War and combat are not pretty, very messy at best. As I reflect on my Vietnam experience, I often think of the following with great compassion, sadness, and humility: 58,148 individuals gave their lives and 75,000 were disabled; of those killed 61% were younger than 21 and 17,539 were married; 240 men were awarded the Medal of Honor. One of those men was S/Sgt Karl Taylor who was my senior drill instructor at Quantico and who has had a very positive impact on my life. He simply taught us to lead by example; he gave his life doing just that.

Bill McEwen

Few had forebodings of their destiny. At the halts they lay in the long wet grass and gossiped. The whistle blew. They jumped for their equipment. The little grey figure of the colonel far ahead waved its stick. Hump your pack and get a move on. The next hour, man, will bring you three hours closer to your death. Your life and your death are nothing to this field-nothing, no more than to the man planning the next attack. You are not even a pawn. Your death will not make the world safe for your children. Your death means no more than if you had died in your bed, full of years and respectability, having begotten a tribe of young. Yet by your courage, you have won the love of those who have watched you. All we remember is your living face and that we loved you for being of our clay and spirit.

Guy Chapman

Few things can help an individual more than to place responsibility on him, and to let him know that you trust him.

Booker t Washington

What was it like to be in Vietnam? What was it like to be at Khe Sanh during the siege and the Tet offensive? Over the years, many people have asked me those questions, especially the one regarding Khe Sanh. I think David Douglas Duncan, a combat photographer who spent eight days with us in February, probably sums it up best: "one adapted quickly to showers of rockets and mortar bombs exploding within the narrow perimeter. It became a life made richer by the common sharing of everyday events: dividing equally the can of a fruit cocktail in a C-ration; tasting a few minutes more of life, helmet-to-helmet in a slit trench with a man who was a stranger before the barrage began-then suddenly he was closer than your brother; watching death roam again among you, and accepting His choice without too deep astonishment that you were once more spared...the battlefield is a world of final simplicity."

Bill McEwen

But to know is nothing; what you know must become your blood.

Martin Gray

Life balance begins with the breath. Taking it all in and letting it all go are the primal rhythms of life. Breathing in, you find inspiration; breathing out , you find release. Inspiring and expiring- birth and death with every breath.

Bill McEwen

Time is really a paradox, stretching between a "past" and a "future" that have no reality except in our own minds. The idea of time is a convention of thought and language, a social agreement. To me a far deeper truth and natural law is simply the following: we have only this moment.

Bill McEwen

In a study done by the American Psychological Association, 69% of employees report that work is a significant source of stress. And 41% say they typically feel tense or stressed out during the day. In a culture that typically defines success as money and power, it seems as if we're stuck on a treadmill of stress, burnout, and frustration.

Bill McEwen

The majority of prescription drugs work on fewer than half the people who take them.

Jeffrey Bland

The world of nature moves in rhythms, patterns, and cycles-the passing of the seasons, the movement of the stars, the ebb and flow of the tides. The seasons do not push one another; neither do the clouds race the wind across the

True North

sky. All things happen in their own good time- rising and falling and rising like ocean waves, in the circles of time.

Unknown

In every winter's heart lies a quivering spring, and behind the veil of each night waits a smiling dawn.

Kahil Gibran

Some think it's holding on that makes one strong; sometimes it's letting go.

Sylvia Robinson

For there can be no boundary between one's self and the others. He who thinks that his self is the unique center of the world, who refuses to see that he is one among all men, will one day know extreme misery and barrenness.

Martin Gray

True North

Many people who have studied on a university level have attained graduate degrees and worldly success find that there is still something missing in their lives. Although they think high thoughts and are intellectually sophisticated, their hearts are still filled with pettiness and doubt. It's like a vulture: it flies high, but what does it feed on?

Ajahn Chah

In my experience, nothing flushes out our reactivity more dramatically than relationships, especially the most intimate ones. Our reactions have a tendency to be mechanical and have been conditioned by years of programming and scripting. Mostly we look, listen, and speak with yesterday's eyes, ears, and voice, often believing that our reflexive and dramatic reactions are a sign of spontaneity.

Bill McEwen

The idea of an "ecological unconsciousness" now hovers above the crossroads of science, philosophy, and theology- the notion that all of nature is connected in ways that we do not fully understand.

Richard Louv

True North

Nature is the ultimate anti-depressant.

Dianne Thomas

Here's an exercise for you: go outside for a walk and pick out anything. It could be a plant, a bird, a tree, a leaf. See if you can look at it for a few minutes without labeling it, naming it, judging, or thinking about it. Simply, with innocence and if for the first time, just take a look at and connect.

Bill McEwen

Creative genius is not the accumulation of knowledge; it is the ability to see patterns in the universe, to detect hidden links between what is and what could be.

Richard Louv

In this writing I have sometimes hit a wall and have run out of things to say. Then I go outside for a walk turning everything loose, and the ideas and words begin to materialize again. It's as if the book is writing me and not the other way around.

Bill McEwen

Wilderness to the people of America is a spiritual necessity, an antidote to the high pressure of modern life, a means of regaining serenity and equilibrium.

Sigurd Olson

Here's my definition of nature: human beings exist in nature anywhere they experience meaningful kinship with other species. By this description, a natural environment may be found in wilderness or in a city; while not required to be pristine, this nature is influenced at least as much by a modicum of wildness and weather as by developers, scientists, beer drinkers, or debutantes. We know this nature when we see it.

Richard Louv

Many times in my life, I have made the following statement: "let's don't violate the process." Process will transform any journey into a series of small steps if taken one by one and will allow us to reach most any goal. Process transcends time, teaches patience, rests on a solid foundation, and embodies trust. And in the writing this book, all of the above have been reinforced.

Bill McEwen

In everyone's life, at some time, our inner fire goes out. It is then burst into flame by an encounter with another human being. We should all be thankful for those people who rekindle the inner spirit.

Albert Schweitzer

Sometimes the only way for me to find out what it is I want to do is to go ahead and do something. Then the moment I start to act, my feelings become clear. It's amazing what movement and action can do for uncertainty.

Bill McEwen

True North

I'm not trying to degrade love but rather to enhance it by elevating these momentary experiences that we typically have trivialized. If we use the word rapport or say, "we clicked," or, "there was real energy there," we might not recognize the true power in such a moment.

Barbara Fredrickson

Love comes in many forms, some of them small. Instead of being a high hurdle, love can be an easy thing to experience. Smile at somebody and see where it leads. Maybe you'll realize that it feels good and you've been missing out.

Barbara Fredrickson

No one is wrong. At most someone is uninformed. If I think an individual is wrong, either I am unaware of something, or he is. So unless I want to play a superiority game I had best find out what he is seeing. "Seek first to understand"…

Bill McEwen

True North

When you are inspired by some great purpose, some extraordinary project, and all your thoughts break their bonds, your mind transcends limitations, your consciousness expands in every direction, and you find yourself in a new, great, and wonderful world, dormant forces, faculties, and talents become alive, and you discover yourself to be a greater person by far than you ever dreamed yourself to be.

Patanjali

How can I tell the difference between what ego is telling me and what my heart is telling me to do? Egocentricity is having a better idea about how this moment should be. Ego talks in terms of "this is right"...this is wrong"...I have to do this...a person must." When we are listening to egocentricity we have the feeling that we know beyond doubt how we should be operating and how life should be. Our heart doesn't tell us what to do. Being at one with our heart simply means being present to and appropriate in the given circumstances. Following the voice of our heart is very subtle. It is so subtle that we have been trained or have trained ourselves not to hear it.

Cheri Huber

True North

Integrity has no need of rules.

Albert Camus

I think that one of life's greatest illusions is the belief that the past is responsible for the current conditions of our lives. We often assign this reason to explain why we can't get out of our ruts. We take the circumstances we experienced in the past, bond ourselves to them, and continue to blame those unfortunate events for our current miserable state. We are living the illusion that our past history is driving our lives.

Bill McEwen

The corporate ladder, the ladder of life, and social strata seem to occupy a big hunk of our life. Do you think, truly, that what is up there is going to be so much more meaningfully different than where you are right now?

Arthur Rosenfield

True North

A new study on Marines during pre-deployment concludes that mindfulness improves working memory, reduces negative emotions, and also reduces stress. If mindfulness regimens can help Marines make better decisions during times of great stress, what might it do for firefighters, police, and the rest of us?

Sharon Begley

I always tell my classes to "never believe anything that I say." It is only when you experience something for yourself that it becomes real. If I don't take what I read or what I am told and weigh it against my own experience, then of what value am I to myself?

Bill McEwen

It has been my experience that rebelling against the forces of attachment within my own heart and mind has been the most revolutionary thing I've ever done. We are addicted to pleasure, in part because we confuse pleasure with happiness. We could all say that deep down, all we want is to be happy. Yet we don't have a realistic understanding of what happiness really is. Happiness is closer to the experience of acceptance and contentment than it is to pleasure. True happiness exists in the spacious and compassionate heart's willingness to feel whatever is present.

Noah Levine

True North

Without a big picture, the inevitable changes in life can overwhelm us. It pays us to remember that when we lose a job or win a promotion, end a marriage, have a grandchild, witness a death, get sick or get well, it's not just personal. It is the dance of life. Always look for the broad perspective.

Bill McEwen

And speaking of that broad perspective, I must share one of my favorite passages which has been very meaningful to me, especially when I get caught up in "my stuff." The following was written by Sylvia Boorstein: "My favorite photo is earthrise as seen from the moon. It's perfect. A great blue and green ball floating in vast black space, hanging right there in its orbit. From that vantage point, the scene on earth is awesome. Creatures are being born, other ones dying; plants are blooming on one side, plants are withering on the other; snow falling, winds howling, volcanoes erupting, earthquakes shivering, people talking, music playing. From the moon's view, it's an incredible cosmic drama. However, from our usual view, inside the drama, looking up at the moon, it's a different story. It changes from THE drama to MY drama and gets to be a problem. If you're far enough away, it's not your story-it's one of the six and a half billion stories. Remembering the two views SIMULTANEOUSLY is a great challenge."

Bill McEwen

True North

What if we all lived our lives as if everything we did would eventually be known?

Bill McEwen

There is no reality except the one contained within us. That is why so many people live such an unreal life. They take the images outside them for reality and never allow the world within the body and mind to reveal itself.

Herman Hesse

As I write this in June of 2014, an Islamic extremist army is on its way to Baghdad, filling ditches with Shiite bodies. Many who advocate military action are clamoring to "do something." Others who have given up on that part of the world are responding "do nothing." One has to marvel at the certainty of those who believe that our next move is so obvious. After a not-so good track record of misjudgments, political maneuvering, bloodshed, and unintended consequences (Vietnam, Haiti, and Afghanistan just to name a few), one has to wonder if there is any decision that we won't come to regret.

Bill McEwen

Your brain is like any other organ in the body- it's designed to adapt constantly. The brain is not static; it's meant to change. The brain keeps changing over its entire lifetime, and you can train it to make those changes. Those changes are now measurable, and new ways of thinking can change it for the better.

Richie Davidson

Wisdom knows what feelings are present without being lost in them.

Jack Kornfield

Our lives, for the most part, are strung out between the thirst for pleasure and the fear of pain. We pass our days running after the one and running away from the other, seldom enjoying the peace of real contentment; real satisfaction seems somehow always out of reach, just beyond the next horizon. Then in the end we have to die: to give up the identity we spent our whole life building, to leave behind everything and everyone we love.

Bhikkhu Bodhi

Wisdom helps us to correct the distorting work of ignorance. It enables us to grasp things as they are in actuality, directly and immediately, free from the screen of ideas, views, and assumptions our minds ordinarily set up between themselves and the real.

Bhikkhu Bodhi

The only thing that threatens you is that of which you are ignorant...pain, death, sickness, loneliness, life, rejection etc.

Cheri Huber

This may have been said before, but it bears repeating; perhaps I'll say it in a different way! My perceptions and my views determine my actions. They lie behind all my choices and goals, and my efforts to turn those choices from ideals into actuality. These actions themselves might determine consequences, but the actions along with their consequences hinge on my views from which they spring. In any situation, if I don't have the right view going in, I can't expect a positive outcome on the other side.

Bill McEwen

There is so much sameness in ordinary life. We are always experiencing everything through the same set of lenses. Once greed, hatred, and delusion are gone, you see everything fresh and new all the time. Every moment is new. Life was dull before. Now, every day, every moment is full of taste and zest.

Dipa Ma

You only arrive at the other shore when you finally realize that there is no other shore. In other words, we make a journey to the "promised land," the other shore, and we have arrived when we realize that we were there all along. It is very paradoxical.

Chogyam Trungpa

True North

You are just living in a small corner of your being -the tiny conscious mind. It is as if somebody has a palace and has completely forgotten about the palace and has started living on the porch- and thinks this is all.

Osho

Two roads diverged in a yellow wood, and sorry I could not travel both and be one traveler, long I stood and looked down one as far as I could to where it bent in the undergrowth...I shall be telling this with a sigh somewhere ages and ages hence: two roads diverged in a wood, and I- I took the one less traveled by, and that has made all the difference.

Robert Frost

Every now and then go away, have a little relaxation, for when you come back to your work, your judgement will be surer; since to remain constantly at work will cause you to lose power of judgement... Go some distance away because the work appears smaller and more of it can be taken in at a glance, and lack of harmony or proportion is more readily seen.

Leonardo Da Vinci

True North

Ultimately nobody can get more out of things including books, than he already knows.

Nietzsche

Everyone knows that there is within him a voice that speaks; it is a simple, clear voice that too often he stifles. For it is a demanding voice, strict as a straight line. This voice, this source that we silence, speaks the truth and gives the means to achieve the equilibrium and liberty of the self. But we are afraid to be ourselves.

Martin Gray

All streams flow to the ocean because it is lower than they are. Humility gives it its power.

Lao Tzu

True North

Someday, after we have mastered the winds, the waves, the tide and gravity, we shall harness for God the power of love. Then, for the second time in the history of the world, man will have discovered fire.

Teilhard De Chardin

Great spirits have always encountered violent opposition from mediocre minds.

Albert Einstein

I have observed the power of the watermelon seed. It has the power of drawing from the ground and through itself 200,000 times its weight. When you can tell me how it takes this material and out of it colors an outside surface beyond the imitation of art, and then forms inside of it a white rind and within that again a red heart, thickly inlaid with black seeds, each one of which is capable of drawing through itself 200,000 times it weight- when you can explain to me the mystery of a watermelon, you can ask me to explain the mystery of God.

William Jennings Bryan

True North

The more I can maintain awareness and mindfulness during the day, tune in to myself to see if what I'm doing is what I want to be doing, then the less I feel at the end of the day that I have been wasting time. But if I "waste time" in awareness and mindfulness, that's o.k.!

Bill McEwen

The art of living...is neither careless drifting on the one hand nor fearful clinging to the past... on the other. It consists of being sensitive to each moment, in regarding it as utterly new and unique, in having the mind open and wholly receptive.

Alan Watts

To practice, we must start exactly where we are. Of course, we can always imagine perfect conditions, how it should be ideally, how everyone else should behave. But it's not out task to create an ideal. It's our task to see how it is and how to learn from the world as it is. For the awakening of the heart, conditions are always good enough.

Ajahn Sumedho

True North

Hills are always more beautiful than stone buildings, you know. Living in a city is an artificial existence. Lots of people hardly ever feel real soil under their feet, see plants grow except in flower pots, or get far enough beyond the street light to catch the enchantment of a night sky studded with stars. When people live far from the great scenes of the Great Spirit's making, it's easy for them to forget his laws.

Walking Buffalo

Every time I step out on my deck or go out in the yard, I can feel the direction of the breeze; I can feel what the animals feel. They can feel the sun rise and the sun set. The plants point in one direction when it is wet and then the other direction when it is dry. It's about connecting the dots…simple as that.

Bill McEwen

We define who we are by what we accept and reject. And your definition of who you are is your prison. You can set yourself free at any time you choose.

Cheri Huber

True North

If you told me when I first arrived in New York City, to start working in network news that I'd be using meditation to defang the voice in my head, I would have laughed at you...Until recently, I thought of meditation as the exclusive province of bearded swamis, unwashed hippies, and fans of John Tesh...I figured it was something that I could never do anyway. I assumed, given the constant looping, buzzing, and fizzing of my thoughts, "that clearing my mind" wasn't an option.

Dan Harris

Mindfulness and meditation is the best story I've ever covered. And I think it's under-covered. There's a revolution brewing. Highly effective people and organizations are using meditation to become better at focusing on their actual work, and responding better to their emotions. Too often, though, mindfulness is talked about in a touchy-feely way that's off-putting to a lot of skeptics. To help change that, would make me very happy.

Dan Harris

No one wants to suffer the penalties that come from living a divided life. But there can be no greater suffering than living a lifelong lie. As we move closer to the truth that

True North

lives within us-aware that in the end what will matter most is knowing that we stayed true to ourselves - institutions start losing their sway over our lives.

Parker Palmer

The best chance we have to address many of the world's issues successfully is to find ways to cultivate some MENTAL SPACE. When leaders make choices that are harmful to an organization, its employees, or the community, it's not due to a lack of IQ: most often, it's the result of an overtaxed schedule and an autopilot existence that leads to careless or reactive decisions

Janice Marturano

Private victories precede public victories. You can't invert that process any more than you can harvest a crop before you plant it.

Stephen Covey

A culture of discipline is not a principle of business. It is a principle of greatness.

Jim Collins

True North

Yesterday I was clever so I wanted to change the world. Today I am wise, so I'm changing myself.

Rumi

Try to see a fast moving light in the night sky, like a meteor or a comet. You have to be alert and look closely. This is how you look at your life as it moves along day by day, trying to catch a glimpse of the purpose in your struggles and suffering. You have to be ready for the unexpected in order to catch a hint of those moving, purpose filled signs. Be ready to accept the many things that happen regularly that are not in your plans, the mistakes that may have meaning for you. This is a particular way of living in which you are not stuck on your plans and expectations and are ready to deal positively and quickly with things that go wrong.

Thomas Moore

Over the last couple of years, I have been very slowly and methodically getting rid of a lot of my "stuff." I'm still in the process, but the clutter is much less than it was a year ago. It's a great way to really practice "letting go"...the trick is to simply start!

Bill McEwen

True North

How different our lives are when we really know what is deeply important to us, and keeping that picture in mind, we manage ourselves each day to be and to do what matters most.

Stephen Covey

No matter what I feel or know, no matter what my potential gifts or talents, only action will bring them to life. When I DO something it usually leads to understanding, and the ACTION usually turns knowledge into wisdom. If not and at some point, the lesson gets repeated!

Bill McEwen

In the second half of life, we do not have strong and final opinions about everything, every event, or most people, as much as we allow things and people to delight us, sadden us, and truly influence us. We no longer need to change or adjust other people to be happy ourselves. Ironically, we are more than ever before in a position to change people-but we do not need to- and that makes all the difference. We have moved from doing to being, to an utterly new kind of doing that flows organically, quietly, and by osmosis. We do what we are called to do, and then try to let go of the consequences. We usually cannot do that very well in youth.

Richard Rohr

All religions are like different cars all moving in the same direction. People who don't see it that way have no light in their hearts.

Ajahn Chah

Love is patient and kind; love is not jealous or boastful; it is not arrogant or rude.

1 Corinthians

All spiritual disciplines are done with a view to still the mind. The perfectly still mind is universal spirit.

Swami Ramdas

True North

Better indeed is knowledge than mechanical practice. Better than knowledge is meditation. But better still is surrender of attachment to results, because there follows immediate peace.

Sri Krishna

The tree which moves some to tears of joy is in the eyes of others only a green thing that stands in the way.

William Blake

Smart people instinctively understand the danger of entrusting our future to self-serving leaders who use our institutions, whether in the corporate or social sector, to advance their own interests.

Jim Collins

When trust is sufficient, laws are unnecessary. When trust is insufficient, laws are unenforceable.

Stephen M. R. Covey

True North

Trust always affects two outcomes-speed and cost. When trust goes down, speed will also go down and costs will go up. On the other hand, when trust goes up, speed will also go up and costs will go down. It's that simple, that real, and that predictable.

Stephen M. R. Covey

I've often thought long and hard about the above passage. How much do you think that a lack of trust is costing this nation every day? How much could we reduce our national debt by simply working on these trust issues at all levels of our society? Our distrust is costing us dearly and has become very expensive. Gandhi said it best: "the moment there is suspicion about a person's motives, everything he does becomes tainted."

Bill McEwen

True North

Mind is the forerunner of all things. Speak or act with an impure mind, and suffering follows as the wagon wheel follows the hoof of the ox. Mind is the forerunner of all things, speak or act with a peaceful mind, happiness follows like a shadow that never leaves.

The Buddha

Walking is the exercise that needs no gym. It is the prescription without medicine, the weight control without diet, the cosmetic that is sold in no drugstore. It is the tranquilizer without a pill, the therapy without a psychoanalyst, and the fountain of youth that is no legend. A walk is the vacation that does not cost a cent.

Aaron Sussman and Ruth Goode

A man on foot, on horseback, or on a bicycle will see more, feel more, and enjoy more in one mile than the motorized tourist can in a hundred miles.

Edward Abbey

True North

As compared to humans, other animals in a constant and mostly unmediated relation with their sensory surroundings think with their whole bodies.

David Abram

It takes a bit of time to create a gap between being a witness and the mind. But once the gap is there, you may be in for a bit of a surprise: you are not your mind; you are the witness, the watcher. What a great way to get rid of all this insanity which was mostly created by your past. We can all do this by just being a witness of our thought processes. It's much like sitting in a theater and watching the scenes come and go on the big screen!

Bill McEwen

As I write this in the summer of 2014 and with all the controversy surrounding the IRS, the VA, Congress, and the current administration, I'm reminded of what someone once said: "it's better to face a cruel truth than continue to live with a comfortable delusion."

Bill McEwen

True North

Remember that self-doubt is as self-centered as self-inflation. Your obligation is to reach as deeply as you can and offer your unique and authentic gifts as bravely and as beautifully as you can.

Bill Plotkin

Speak to the earth, and it shall teach thee.

Job 12:8

In the moment you feel you need to manage someone, you've made a hiring mistake. The best people don't need to be managed. Guided, taught, led-yes. But not managed.

Jim Collins

Where is peace to be found? It's found in the same place as sorrow...How convenient!

Robert Rosenbaum

True North

If I've really done my best, I never fear failure.

Bill McEwen

Live your own life for you will die your own death.

Mike Gaddis

Where are you searching for me, friend? Look! Here I am right within you. Not in a temple, nor in mosque, not in Kaaba, nor Kailas, but here right within you I am.

Kabir

Sin is whatever obscures the soul.

Andrew Gide

Every animal knows far more about nature than I do.

Bill McEwen

True North

Here's the reinforced lesson which my two cancer surgeries along with this current broken ankle have taught me: the universe placed me in good hands; I set my intention; mental and physical conditioning, both pre-and post-operation are extremely important; pain and dependence are wonderful teachers; breath, movement, awareness, and presence were invaluable; finally, my imagination was much more frightening than my reality. If by chance these lessons help one other traveler, this entire book has been worthwhile.

Bill McEwen

Life has a tendency to be messy. I think this is a reality that many individuals tend to ignore. We can never see what's coming until it's arrived, and once something has emerged, we have to work with it. We have to be willing to be flexible and adapt. We can't keep pushing ahead with old views and perceptions, outdated plans, and dreams. Sometimes we have to fall apart before we can figure out how to reorganize ourselves to fit a new environment. Change is just the way it is.

Bill McEwen

True North

I think the following words might accurately describe this particular time on our planet: chaotic; uncertain; turbulent; restless; weird; out of control. Change today is profoundly different in volume, intensity, and consequence than ever before. We have completely changed the experience of change because of global networks of communication. However and at some point, I think that we'll all have to understand that in this universe, relationships are the key. We all live on one small planet, and in the interest of survival, we must find ways to live together. Einstein said it best: "we live in a prison, created by an optical illusion of separateness."

Bill McEwen

One of my caps which I wear on a regular basis has the following inscribed on it: on the front is a small Marine Corps emblem and on the back are the words "RVN- Khe Sanh, 1968. On the inside band are the words "made in Vietnam, one size fits most." Everything changes...I'm reminded of a passage from Ecclesiastes: "there is a time for everything, and a season for every activity under heaven."

Bill McEwen

True North

The fear of death follows from the fear of life. A man who lives fully is prepared to die at any time.

Edward Abbey

People think of the mind as being located in the head, but the latest findings in physiology suggests that the mind doesn't really exist in the brain, but rather travels the whole body on caravans of hormone and enzyme, busily making sense of the compound wonders we usually catalogue as touch, taste, smell, hearing, and vision.

Diane Ackerman

The latest studies suggest that thought isn't limited to the mind or the five senses we thought it was…scientists have discovered conservatively ten and possibly as many as thirty senses (such as the ability to tell time without a watch), senses that awaken, once we spend time in nature…it's all about awareness, what you perceive, sense, and feel in new ways.

Richard Louv

True North

Meditation is a way of being, not a technique.

Jon Kabat-Zinn

Sometimes there is no sense in waiting around for the science to back up something that you already know to be true.

Bill McEwen

Society constantly expends its efforts to correct EFFECTS instead of CAUSES which is one reason why the development of human consciousness proceeds so slowly. Human beings are barely on the first rung of the evolutionary ladder; we haven't yet solved even such primitive problems as world hunger.

David Hawkins

True North

To commit oneself to too many projects, to want to help everyone in everything, is to succumb to the violence of modern times.

Thomas Merton

It may be that when we no longer know what to do that we have come to our real work. And when we no longer know which way to go, only then have we begun our real journey.

Wendell Berry

The basic law of the universe is economy. The universe doesn't waste a single quark; everything serves a purpose and fits into balance- there are no extraneous events.

David Hawkins

True North

Things in the domain of inner and outer experience are workable to an astonishing degree, but much more so and sometimes ONLY if you step up and do the work. It may be the most difficult work in the world, and I for one believe that, when it comes to cultivating mindfulness and tasting freedom from the conditioned mind, it is actually the most difficult work in the world.

Jon Kabat-Zinn

One of my children recently made the following comment to me: "Dad you're out of your mind; do you know that?" And my reply: "Yes, and it's taken me a long time to get there."

Bill McEwen

We shall not cease from exploration and the end of all our exploring will be to arrive where we started and to know that place for the first time.

T.S Eliot

True North

Human behavior has changed very little in the last 2,000 years. What has changed can be summarized in basically two words: speed and options.

Bill McEwen

If is possible to live with a purpose, what should that purpose be? A purpose might be a guiding principle, a philosophy, or an ideal of sovereign importance that informs and directs our actions. To have one is to live seriously (though not necessarily wisely) following some track, seeking in the maze of the world a special goal or an end before which all the hubbub of vanity subsides. What is your purpose, friend, or what should it be?

Bhikkhu Nyanasobhano

Tell me, what is it you plan to do with your one wild and precious life?

Mary Oliver

True North

A change of heart or of values without a practice is only another pointless luxury of a passively consumptive way of life.

Wendell Berry

Man thinks he lives by virtue of what he can control, but in fact, he's governed by power from unrevealed sources, power over which he has no control.

David Hawkins

Worry is a problem that seems to be rampant. Perhaps it is due to the nature of our overly advanced civilization or to the addictions we have to our highly sophisticated technology. The next time you find yourself worrying or getting stressed, consider the following: "When you can do anything, to change your circumstances, why worry about it? When you cannot do anything to change your circumstances, why worry about it?"

Bill McEwen

True North

There are three levels of truth: experience, reasoning, and knowing. All other assertions should be rejected.

Deng Ming-Dao

Don't make the mistake of believing that acceptance and surrender means passive resignation. In fact, quite the opposite is true.

Bill McEwen

Our goals, our vision, our philosophy, whatever you choose to call it are very personal. No one knows us better than we know ourselves. Maybe there should be only one universal goal: a gracious death with no regrets.

Bill McEwen

What makes the world so maddeningly hard to measure is the prevalence here of eight "worldly phenomena": gain and loss; fame and lack of fame; pleasure and pain; praise and blame. These volatile phenomena upset our predictions and our longing for stability, bringing now happiness, now afflictions, oblivious to our welfare; and amid their uproar we labor on wretchedly, trying to separate the desired from the undesired.

Bhikkhu Nyanasobhano

…Actually the masters have already babbled away all the secrets. In their compassionate determination to pass on their insights, they have worn themselves out trying to get their messages across to us. The secrets of life are already written in all the holy books. They are only secrets because we do not take the time to truly read. Can you see the jewels in the mud?

Deng Ming- Dao

One of my big life's lessons: actions undertaken with a pure intent have repercussions throughout the web of life beyond what can be measured or discerned.

Bill McEwen

True North

Times are difficult globally; awakening is no longer a luxury or an ideal. It's becoming critical. We don't need to add more depression, more discouragement, or more anger to what's already here. It's becoming clear that we need to learn how to relate sanely with difficult times. The earth seems to be beseeching us to connect with joy and discover our innermost essence. This is the best way that we can benefit others.

Pema Chodron

We ourselves feel that what we are doing is just a drop in the ocean. But the ocean would be less because of missing that drop.

Mother Teresa

We would never learn to be brave and patient if there were only joy in the world.

Helen Keller

True North

Example is not the main thing in influencing others. It is the only thing.

Albert Schweitzer

Things turn out best for the people who make the best of the way that things turn out.

John Wooden

Really seeking to understand the other person is probably one of the most important Emotional Bank Account deposits that you can make, and it is the key to every other deposit. What is important to the other person must be as important to you as the other person is to you.

Stephen Covey

Here's another one of my big life's lessons. I have found that when I'm truly connected and in a centered state of purpose that I activate forces in the universe that previously may have been out of my range. What I need will show up. The right person will be there on time. This book will be finished when appropriate. The phone call will come. The missing pieces will all begin to fit. All the seemingly coincidences in my life become quite normal.

Bill McEwen

We don't sit in meditation to become good meditators. We sit in meditation so that we'll be more awake in our lives.

Pema Chodron

Adopt the pace of nature; her secret is patience.

Ralph Waldo Emerson

The mind out of control is like a restless monkey jumping here and there senselessly. You have to learn to control it. See the real nature of the mind: impermanent, unsatisfactory, and empty. Don't just follow it as it jumps around. Learn to master it. Chain it down and let it wear itself out and die. Then you have a dead monkey, and you're finally at peace.

Ajahn Chah

True North

Presence has taught me that what I do today is really important, because in effect, I am trading a day of my life for it.

Bill McEwen

Karma means: you don't get away with nothing.

Ruth Denison

Be mindful of intention. Intention is the seed that creates our future.

Jack Kornfield

A basic assumption to which a lot of us cling is the following: I have to MAKE life happen. If I don't, it won't be the way I want it to be. We're so desperately invested in this assumption that we won't risk allowing life simply to be the way it is even for a moment to find out if we would like it. I don't think that this is an accident, because if we really accepted things the way they are and LIKED it, what would our function be? What would we do all day? Since we have a tendency to spend our days trying to CONTROL life, we'd be out of work!

Bill McEwen

The only preparation for death, it turns out, is the moment-to- moment life process. When you live in the present now, and then this present, and then THIS present, when the moment of death comes, you are not living in the future or the past. The freaky thing about death is the anticipatory fear of it. But you can't tell someone else to live in the present moment unless you yourself are.

Ram Dass

Most all creative endeavors are somewhat unpredictable. They often seem ambiguous, hit-or-miss, trial and error. And unless people have a high tolerance for ambiguity and get their security from integrity from principles and inner values, they find it unnerving and unpleasant to be involved in highly creative enterprises. Their need for structure, certainty, and predictability is too high.

Stephen Covey

True North

The good citizen knows that the land is a sacred trust. He feels that when he passes it on to future generations, it must be as good as when he found it or better.

Sigurd Olson

In permanently protecting this sacred piece of land that I often fondly refer to as "my briar patch", I have no doubt that future generations will come to truly appreciate and value all the many blessings that it has to offer.

Bill McEwen

May your trails be crooked, winding, lonesome, danderous leading to the most amazing view. May your mountains rise into and above the clouds.

Edward Abbey

True North

Final Thoughts:

It is indeed one of the big challenges of this era to maintain sanity in an increasingly insane world. How are we ever going to perform at a new level of consciousness if we are continually caught up in all the monkey chatter of our own minds and the bewilderment of feelings lost or isolated or out of touch with what it all means and who we are? Hopefully some of the wisdom in this book has provided some answers. I encourage you not only to reflect but to also apply these teachings in your daily life. The only real way to know is to do. Most of the "True North" teachings in this book did not come from me. They already exist everywhere and are practiced, taught, and embodied by countless generations of men and women, many of whom live among us. All I have done is to simply "pass them forward" and added some of my own personal insights.

In the last part of the 20th century and up until the present, vast amounts of technology and information have characterized our world. So the question now becomes: "What's next?" The following quote may provide a clue: "Where is the wisdom we have lost in knowledge; where is the knowledge we have lost in information?" As we have moved up our evolutionary ladder from hunter/gatherer to our current rung of knowledge and information, I believe that our next step must be into the realm of wisdom, characterized by a fundamental shift in our human consciousness. Hopefully, this small book has shed some light on that "shift."

True North

Finally, there are many unsung heroes and heroines at this critical moment in our collective story. There are so many courageous persons, who unbeknownst to themselves, are holding together this world by their resolute love, by their expanding consciousness, and by their contagious joy. Although I do not know your names, I can feel you out there. Thank you for sharing my journey.

About the Author

Bill holds both a B.S. and M.S. degree from the University of Tennessee in Knoxville. In 1966 after completing Officer's Candidate School in Quantico, Virginia, he was commissioned as an officer in the Marine Corps. During his tour of duty, he served for thirteen months in South Vietnam and was honorably discharged in 1969 as a Captain.

The majority of his professional career was spent at Columbia State Community College where he served in various positions. After retiring in 2007, he continues to share his life experiences on a deeper level by facilitating "Principles of Effectiveness" for both individuals and organizations.

Bill and his wife Shirley live in the small rural community of Duck River, Tennessee where they reside on the family farm.

True North

This book is dedicated to all those explorers on a journey toward a new world, a world evolving from one of information and technology to one of wisdom. This new world is characterized by a new dimension of consciousness.

Cover Art by Stewart Marston

CPSIA information can be obtained at www.ICGtesting.com
Printed in the USA
LVOW04s2341230814

400625LV00005B/6/P